Soul Breakthrough

Soul Breakthrough

Tricia Martin

"Therefore if anyone is in Christ,

he is a new creation."

2 Corinthians 5:17

Cover design by Glenda Hoffman
ISBN (paperback) 9781730980794

SBT
soulbreakthrou.com

Contents

Soul Breakthrough
Class One

Do you want to be free from being ruled by your old ways of thinking and feeling and instead be filled with the Holy Spirit? Do you want to access the resources of heaven when faced with familiar situations that would normally push you back into the old ways of responding?

What Is Soul Breakthrough?

Through the Soul Breakthrough classes, you are inviting the Holy Spirit to come into specific habits, thoughts, and emotions that repeatedly hinder your everyday life. You (and I) have habits from our old lives, before we knew Jesus, that are so familiar we need the Lord to point them out. By the end of this four-week course, new ways of thinking and feeling will be rooted in you as the Holy Spirit partners with you in this change.

Through this teaching and the homework, you will partner with the Holy Spirit in transforming areas that you have not been able to change, old ways of thinking, feeling, and reacting. Now, the Holy Spirit will reprogram those areas and retrain the mind.

You will find you are more aware of the Lord and His heavenly resources in your everyday life, and He will bring His presence into the areas of chaos, fear, and pain at home, at work, in relationships, and at church. By inviting the Holy Spirit to fill you at those times when old familiar thoughts and emotions rule, you will then see the situations differently.

As you learn to bring the Holy Spirit into old ways of thinking and feeling, new habits will be formed as pathways in the brain are transformed. You will receive freedom from chronic anxiety, addictions, PTSD, marriage issues, depression, and trauma as you invite the Holy Spirit into your day. Areas in your emotions and thoughts that are part of the old nature and old system will be brought to the Lord to have the Holy Spirit fill them with His new ways of thinking and feeling. The brain will be reprogrammed by the Holy Spirit in areas that are in *the habit* of reacting in the old ways of thinking and feeling.

You will have a new freedom from old ways of thinking and feeling, a transformation of your mind and emotions by the Holy Spirit, and a new intimacy with God as you practice His presence throughout the day. You will be able to walk into your Promised Land and be free from old thoughts of fear, anxiety, and insecurity.

The Bible teaches us that **if we are a new creation in Christ, then the old has passed away and all things are new.** *Yeah, right*, you might be thinking. Then why don't I *feel* like a new creation?

If you have accepted Jesus Christ as your Savior, then you are a beloved child of God. Many of you have invited the Holy Spirit to come and baptize you with His presence and power. But you may still be experiencing panic attacks, fear, depression, addiction, and other negative responses to life circumstances.

So What Is Going On?

May I suggest that, yes, you are a new creation and have been born again into Father God's kingdom. However, you (and I) have habits from our old lives before we knew Jesus that are so engrained we need the Lord to show them to us. You and I don't know what we don't know, right? We have areas that overwhelm us, distract us from God, and pull us back into fear, depression, anxiety, panic, and many other familiar thoughts and emotions. Sometimes we are not even aware we are functioning in the "old man."

By the end of this four-week course, new patterns of thinking and feeling will be firmly rooted into your thoughts and emotions. As the Holy Spirit partners with you in this process, it will be His

Spirit healing, not you healing yourself through your own efforts, which, by the way, have probably failed over and over, like mine, through the years.

Let's get started on a wonderful journey with the Father, Son, and Holy Spirit, and allow them to set us free to walk in new patterns of thinking and feeling. Remember: **We are a new creation in Christ. The old has passed away, and everything is new.**

> **Therefore, if anyone *is* in Christ, he *is* a new creation; old things have passed away; behold, all things have become new. (2 Corinthians 5:17 NKJV)**

Soul Breakthrough, What It Is and What It Isn't

This class is not about counseling, inner healing, breaking soul ties, or deliverance. The truth is many of us have had years of sermons, worship, prayer, healing, counseling, and other people pouring into our lives. This class is about *standing* in the new creation that we received when we were born again and walking with the Lord into our Promised Land.

Once you have learned how to do this, it will become natural. You will even find that you are walking in the Spirit at times when you would have previously reacted in the old ways of the soul with fear, anxiety, anger, insecurity, or addictions ruling you. Now you will respond in the new nature with the Holy Spirit and see your circumstances through His eyes!

As you learn to bring the Holy Spirit into troubling areas, new pathways will begin to form inside your brain, establishing new habits. In practicing this new way of thinking and feeling, you will become increasingly aware that Father God, Jesus, and the Holy Spirit are always there with you, moment by moment. Repetition is the **key.**

What, then, is the final accomplishment? You will become who God created you to be. As your old nature and old system are transformed by the Lord, the Holy Spirit supernaturally will break old habits that you have been unsuccessful in breaking before. You will be filled with His new ways of thinking and feeling. No longer will you be drained and ruled by the "old man," but instead through the Holy Spirit, you will choose to access the resources of heaven in those same situations that would have taken you into the old, negative thoughts and emotions.

My story

Several years ago, I was given a prophetic word that I would develop a new teaching called *Soul Breakthrough* and that it would simplify to God's children how to invite the Holy Spirit into their everyday lives in such a way as to transform areas in their minds and emotions. Through this teaching I would be partnering with the Lord to help bring people out of the wilderness and into their Promised Land.

God's precious children would be set free from addiction, PTSD, chronic anxiety, marriage problems, depression, and so many other things that plagued them. They would learn to invite the Lord into their daily, moment-by-moment lives, and become filled with His Spirit. This teaching would spread rapidly as people began to walk in this Spirit-led lifestyle.

The person who gave me this word, then asked me if there was something in my own life that caused me to react in the old man and not by the Spirit. I couldn't think of anything major at that time, but about a week later, the Holy Spirit made me aware of a recurring situation that I have had with extended family for twenty to twenty-five years. It seems that every few months at least one of my family members is hospitalized or has a major crisis of some sort. One month I had six family members in the hospital at the same time: one had attempted suicide, another had been placed in a psychiatric hospital, a third in a regular hospital and three elderly parents had been hospitalized all in the same month.

The interesting thing about all of this is because it had been going on for such a long time and had become **so familiar,** I needed the Holy Spirit to reveal to me my patterns of responding. I would react in feelings of heaviness, tiredness, anxiety and feeling overwhelmed. I realized at this point that I was feeling inadequate to handle these traumatic, stressful situations continually presented to my husband and me.

I was showed a new way of inviting the Holy Spirit, Jesus, and Father God into these overwhelming circumstances. And guess what? Now when there is a crisis in my extended family, I don't fall back into the broken old ways of thinking and feeling, but instead feel the Holy Spirit's presence and remember the heavenly resources I have available. My husband and I are able to respond in the new ways of the Spirit.

Recently, several family members were hospitalized. In the past, I would have reacted in feelings of heaviness, tiredness, worry, and inadequacy to help them. But now, I lift my hands and invite the Father to come and fill me up. I am able to look at the situation from a heavenly perspective and be led by the Holy Spirit. He shined His light on this family issue and filled my familiar place of brokenness with His Spirit and His peace. The Lord retrained my thinking and created a new Spirit-filled "track" in my mind and emotions.

In *Soul Breakthrough,* you will learn how to invite the Holy Spirit, throughout your day, into the broken areas of your soul that will enable you to respond as the new creation you were called to be in Jesus. As you receive these principles and apply them in everyday life, with the help of the Holy Spirit and practice, **they will become habits**. You can then step into who God called you to be, and find freedom from fear, addiction, panic, depression, and whatever other habits are still plaguing you.

Accessing What Is Already Ours

Imagine that you broke your leg and the Lord sovereignly healed it. But you still, out of habit, continue to limp around, forgetting that your leg was healed. Slipping back into old habits is the equivalent of forgetting your leg is healed and continuing to limp. This is how we often walk in our daily lives. When a crisis occurs, we tend to forget all the wonderful things the Lord has done for us and all the areas in our lives He has healed. We forget that we are new creations in Him, filled with His Spirit and with access to every resource available in heaven.

Beloved, let us choose to stand in our healing and the new creation we are in God. Let's invite the Holy Spirit to immediately move into those thoughts and emotions that have been restored, and not allow old habits of thinking or feeling to move us back into our old nature. It is time to step fully into who we are called to be, walking moment-by-moment with His Spirit.

Look at the scriptures below:

> **Not that I have already obtained this or am already perfect, but I press on to make it my own, because Christ Jesus has made me His own. Brothers, I do not consider that I have made it my own. But one thing I do: forgetting what lies behind and straining forward to what lies ahead, I press on toward the goal for the prize of the upward call of God in Christ Jesus. (Philippians 3:12-14)**

> **Therefore, since we are surrounded by so great a cloud of witnesses, let us also lay aside every weight, and sin which clings so closely, and let us run with endurance the race that is set before us. (Hebrews 12:1)**

In these scriptures, the apostle Paul is referring to "the race" we entered when we accepted Jesus Christ as our Savior. He uses the Greek games as an illustration because they were very influential and a major part of the culture of his time. Paul lived for eighteen months in Corinth, and he was amazed at the amount of time and effort the Greek athletes put into these games to win a simple olive wreath.

Paul, however, wanted the Christians in Corinth to concentrate on a different type of competition—one far greater than the Olympic Games—a *spiritual* race with the final reward being the Kingdom of God and eternal life. Paul emphasized the importance of finishing this spiritual race with victory.

My Vision

When I began to understand the principles of Soul Breakthrough, I had a vision. I saw myself running in a race with a large group of people who were very close to completing this season of our lives. The Lord was beside us, encouraging us to run through the finish line. However, the enemy had set up smoke and mirrors that completely covered the finish line so we could not see it; it was hidden.

Jesus wants us, by faith, to run right through the smoke and mirrors into the new season He has for each of us. Beloved, we are so much closer to moving into this new and amazing season than the enemy wants us to believe. Jesus is offering to transform our minds and emotions so we can move into His healing and His new nature.

Our Broken Soul Transformed by God

After graduating from high school, I moved out of my mother's home and drove a couples of hours south to San Diego State University to attend college. At that school, I received a bachelor's degree in psychology and then a master's degree in counseling from National University.

I chose this field of study because for years I had watched my mother counsel and minister hope and healing to people in emotional pain and brokenness. I then began working as a marriage and family counselor for several years until I observed that people were not really changing or being set free through the training I had received.
Some of what I learned through psychology didn't work for Christians because it was focused on a person's ability to fix

themselves. As born-again new creations, we have a completely different orientation to healing; we invite God to renew our old ways of thinking and feeling. Partnering with our Creator, we receive His healing and transformation.

We Are Made up of Three Parts:

Each and every human is made up of three parts. We have a spirit, a soul (which is comprises of our mind, emotions, and will), and we have a body. Before accepting Jesus, we made all of our decisions through our soul based on our thoughts and feelings.

The problem is our minds are similar to a computer in that that they can be programmed. Once programmed, they continue to function that way **until we reprogram them.**

Before salvation, our minds processed everything through our past experience. For example, when evaluating a situation, we might have thought, *will this situation cause more pain, or will this situation cause safety and pleasure?* Our parents borrowed their negative belief systems (lies) from their parents, and the decisions our parents made were based on avoiding hurt and pain. And now their belief system has become ours.

Our brains have been in the habit of repetitively operating out of the familiarity of fear and rejection. We are so accustomed to thinking and feeling in these old patterns that many times we no longer have an awareness of our reactions in various situations. The Holy Spirit is then needed to reveal these areas to us so we can partner with Him and step out of our old, familiar patterns and into the new creation we are in Christ.

Why Do We Hurt Ourselves and Others?

Through different circumstances and crises along our journey in life, our minds have become wounded and programed to distrust. Inevitably, when we expected good things to happen to us, they didn't. When our expectations were not met, we felt rejection, and that emotion embedded itself into our souls, storing that event of fear or hurt deep inside our brain. In wanting to feel safe and secure, we placed our trust and identity into our work, ministry, school, money, friends, family, title, position, and areas of talented or giftedness—anything that would bring a sense of security and rest.

From childhood, our minds were taught worldly truth that was contrary to God's kingdom. As a result, our misunderstanding of His truth wounded our brain, along with trauma and sin, and significant people in our lives injuring us. All of these factors caused us to unconsciously build a wall of protection.

God wants to free us from the false identities given to us by those around us. Our true identity is not from our father, mother, sibling, spouse, friends, job, ministry, money—none of these are life giving. We can now partner with the Holy Spirit in consciously pulling down thoughts, attitudes, and emotions from our old nature and replacing them with the new thoughts, attitudes and emotions that lie within the new creation that is our inheritance.

Our Father Assures Us of His Love!

Father God reminds us that we are His sons and daughters and that He accepts us. The Father, the Son, and the Holy Spirit live within us, so we are no longer ruled by our broken soul but by the power and fruit of the Spirit. Within us is a new value system from heaven, and He is the center. We are being led by the Holy Spirit. We can believe this by faith!

Every day, every moment, we have a choice. The battle is in choosing the new creation that we have been born into—or our old nature. Sometimes our habits are so familiar we are unaware of them without the help of the Holy Spirit.

His Freedom Lifestyle

Beloved, let's say *yes* to living lives led by the Holy Spirit. We can choose to align ourselves with the Holy Spirit and welcome His presence throughout our day, every day. Nothing outside us can dictate who we are because we have been born again by God.

By becoming aware of the Lord and His heavenly resources in our everyday lives, we can bring His presence into the areas of chaos, fear, and pain at home, at work, in our relationships, and at church. **Faith is the key**. We accepted Jesus by faith; our sins were forgiven by faith; and we have been filled with the Holy Spirit by faith. When we invite God to fill us during the day, we need faith to believe that we will receive His Spirit when we ask. Remember Jesus said, **"Ask and it will be given." (Matthew 7:7).**

What Is the Key? Changing Our Old Ways of Thinking and Feeling.

The Holy Spirit can renew and fill our minds and emotions to help us respond afresh to situations that previously caused us to react in fear, insecurity, and frustration, which stole our peace. At any moment we can invite Him to come and break that old way of thinking, filling us with His presence. Don't forget He is inside you.

The Kingdom of God is within you. (Luke 17:21 KJV)

Become aware of the peace and resources that heaven makes available to us at all times. The enemy of our souls works against us to pull us back into old patterns of thinking and feeling, in order to make us forget who we are—a new creation in Christ. If we are continually aware of what we have in the Spirit—His peace and joy, then we have intimacy with Him.

Awareness of What Is Controlling Us.

It's easy to focus on and be filled with God at church, when listening to worship music, or in a Christian setting. But what happens when a serious problem threatens to overwhelm us and we face it daily at home or away from our church family? What are our reactions to being frightened by something or receiving bad news about finances, health, or our family?

It is critical that we invite the Spirit of God into these difficult times and look at them from a heavenly perspective. The Spirit will help us to identify what is controlling us at these times. Is it anger, fear, stress, anxiety, offense, depression, or insecurity? It is at these times that we move out of our Promised Land and move back into the wilderness of old thoughts and feeling. We fall back into our broken belief systems and lies that we learned from parents and other people in our lives, and look at life through these old, broken belief systems.

Accessing the Resources of Heaven.

Therefore, if anyone is in Christ, he is a new creation. The old has passed away; behold the new has come. (2 Corinthians 5:17)

What if we were to invite the Holy Spirit to fill us in those times when the old familiar thoughts and emotions were ruling us? We would begin to see our situations differently through the Spirit. We would see that we have every resource in heaven and that we are a friend of God. When we stop and invite Him into the daily situations of our lives and give Him permission to make us aware of how we are reacting, old patterns and ways of thinking are disrupted, and new tracks begins to form in our minds and emotions. If we do this every day for several weeks, then circuits in our brains begin to change and create new ways of thinking and feeling. Old habits are broken by the Holy Spirit and new ways of thinking and feeling develop.

The apostle Paul said to "walk by the Spirit." The Creator of all things wants to fill us with new life, new ways of thinking, and new ways of seeing and feeling.

Let's Start the Process

Each day before the next class, commit to doing the steps below. Remember: repetition is the key to your Soul Breakthrough!

Homework:

Simple ways to train the brain through the Holy Spirit.

This week, **each morning**, invite the Holy Spirit to show you during the day when you are thinking and feeling the old broken ways. Give the Holy Spirit permission, during your day, to make you **aware** of what is controlling you.

When you are in a situation where you feel controlled by fear, anger, stress, depression, or insecurity, then lift your hands to Father God and say, "Father, fill me with your Holy Spirit now. **I choose** to turn from anger, fear, stress, depression, _____to focus on you." Take a deep breath and count to four. Now look at the situation filled with His Spirit and from the new creation that you are, and you will see things differently.

You have every resource in heaven, and you are a friend of God. Combine the physical act of lifting your hands while you invite the Holy Spirit into your thoughts and emotions. This will break the old ways of thinking so you can focus on the infilling of God. You can choose any physical act to combine with your words: clapping, smiling, looking up to heaven, or closing your eyes.

During the day, be aware that the Holy Spirit is there with you constantly. Repetition reminds your brain of this, and the brain will acknowledge it and gradually change the pathways and create new tracks of thinking.

Day 1

1. Invite Father God into your day and give the Holy Spirit permission to make you aware when you begin to move into old ways of thinking and feeling in response to familiar triggers. Then breathe deeply and lift your hands and invite Father God to fill you with His presence. Now journal what the Holy Spirit is saying to you.

2. Read several scriptures (feel free to read the scriptures below listed at the end of day seven).

3. Pray in your spiritual language for fifteen minutes. If you do not have a spiritual language (the gift of tongues), then listen to worship music and sing to the Lord for fifteen minutes.

For those of you not sure what "praying in your spiritual language" means, I am referring to one of the nine gifts of the Holy Spirit, the gift of tongues, shown in Acts 2:1-4:

> When the day of Pentecost arrived, they were all together in one place. And suddenly there came from heaven a sound like a mighty rushing wind, and it filled the entire house where they were sitting. And divided tongues as of fire appeared to them and rested on each one of them. And they were all filled with the Holy Spirit and began to speak in other tongues as the Spirit gave them utterance.

Paul took the road through the interior and arrived at Ephesus. There he found some disciples and asked them, "Did you receive the Holy Spirit when you believed?" They answered, "No, we have not even heard that there is a Holy Spirit." So Paul asked, "Then what baptism did you receive?" "John's baptism," they replied. Paul said, "John's baptism was a baptism of repentance. He told the people to believe in the one coming after him, that is, in Jesus." On hearing this, they were baptized in the name of the Lord Jesus. When Paul placed his hands on them, the Holy Spirit came on them, and they spoke in tongues and prophesied. (Acts 19:1-6)

I thank God that I speak in tongues more than all of you. Nevertheless, in church I would rather speak five words with my mind in order to instruct others, than ten thousand words in a tongue. (1 Corinthian 14:18-19)

Anyone who speaks in a tongue edifies themselves, but the one who prophesies edifies the church. (1 Corinthians 14:4)

A few more scriptures on this for further study are Acts 19:6, 1 Corinthians 12:8-10, and 1 Corinthians 12:4, 21, 22.

Journal_____

_____

_____

_____

_____

_____

_____

_____

_____

_____

_____

_____

Day 2

1. Invite Father God into your day and give the Holy Spirit permission to make you aware when you begin to move into old ways of thinking and feeling in response to familiar triggers. Then breathe deeply and lift your hands and invite Father God to fill you with His presence. Now journal what the Holy Spirit is saying to you.

2. Read several scriptures (feel free to read the scriptures below listed at the end of day seven).

3. Pray in your spiritual language for fifteen minutes or listen to worship music and sing to the Lord for fifteen minutes.

Journal_____

_____

_____

_____

_____

_____

_____

_____

_____

_____

_____

Day 3

1. Invite Father God into your day and give the Holy Spirit permission to make you aware when you begin to move into old ways of thinking and feeling in response to familiar triggers. Then breathe deeply and lift your hands and invite Father God to fill you with His presence. Now journal what the Holy Spirit is saying to you.

2. Read several scriptures (feel free to read the scriptures below listed at the end of day seven).

3. Pray in your spiritual language for fifteen minutes or listen to worship music and sing to the Lord for fifteen minutes.

Journal_____

_____

_____

_____

_____

_____

_____

_____

_____

_____

Day 4

1. Invite Father God into your day and give the Holy Spirit permission to make you aware when you begin to move into

old ways of thinking and feeling in response to familiar triggers. Then breathe deeply and lift your hands and invite Father God to fill you with His presence. Now journal what the Holy Spirit is saying to you.

2. Read several scriptures (feel free to read the scriptures below listed at the end of day seven).

3. Pray in your spiritual language for fifteen minutes or listen to worship music and sing to the Lord for fifteen minutes.

Journal_____

_____

_____

_____

_____

_____

_____

_____

_____

_____

Day 5

1. Invite Father God into your day and give the Holy Spirit permission to make you aware when you begin to move into old ways of thinking and feeling in response to familiar triggers. Then breathe deeply and lift your hands and invite Father God to fill you with His presence. Now journal what the Holy Spirit is saying to you.

2. Read several scriptures (feel free to read the scriptures below listed at the end of day seven).

3. Pray in your spiritual language for fifteen minutes or listen to worship music and sing to the Lord for fifteen minutes.

Journal_____

_____

_____

_____

_____

_____

_____

_____

_____

_____

_____

Day 6

1. Invite Father God into your day and give the Holy Spirit permission to make you aware when you begin to move into old ways of thinking and feeling in response to familiar triggers. Then breathe deeply and lift your hands and invite Father God to fill you with His presence. Now journal what the Holy Spirit is saying to you.

2. Read several scriptures (feel free to read the scriptures below listed at the end of day seven).

3. Pray in your spiritual language for fifteen minutes or listen to worship music and sing to the Lord for fifteen minutes.

Journal_____

_____

_____

_____

_____

_____

_____

_____

_____

_____

_____

Day 7

1. Invite Father God into your day and give the Holy Spirit permission to make you aware when you begin to move into old ways of thinking and feeling in response to familiar triggers. Then breathe deeply and lift your hands and invite Father God to fill you with His presence. Now journal what the Holy Spirit is saying to you.

2. Read several scriptures (feel free to read the scriptures below listed at the end of day seven).

3. Pray in your spiritual language for fifteen minutes or listen to worship music and sing to the Lord for fifteen minutes.

Journal_____

_____

_____

_____

_____

_____

_____

_____

_____

_____

_____

Daily Scriptures

2 Corinthians 5:17: Therefore if anyone is in Christ, he is a new creation. The old has passed away; behold the new has come.

Jeremiah 29:11: For I know the plans I have for you, declares the Lord, plans to prosper you and not to harm you, plans to give you hope and a future.

Isaiah 26:3: You keep him in perfect peace whose mind is stayed on you, because he trusts in You.

John 10:10: I have come that they may have life and have it to the full.

Exodus 33:14: My Presence will go with you and I will give you rest.

Philippians 4:13: I can do all things through Christ who strengthens me.

Isaiah 41:10: Do not fear, for I am with you; do not be dismayed for I am your God. I will strengthen you and help you; I will uphold you with My righteous right arm.

Proverbs 3:3-6: Trust in the Lord with all your heart, and do not rely on your own understanding. Acknowledge Him in all your ways, and He will make your paths straight.

Romans 8:28: And we know that in all things God works for the good of those who love Him, who have been called according to His purpose.

Matthew 11:29: Come to Me all you who are weary and burdened, and I will give you rest. Take My yoke upon you and learn from Me, for I am gentle and humble in heart and you will find rest for your souls. For My yoke is easy and My burden is light.

Isaiah 44:3-5: I will pour water on the thirsty land, and streams on the dry ground; I will pour out My Spirit on your offspring, and My blessing on your descendants. They shall spring up among the grass like willows by flowing streams. This one will say, 'I am the LORD's…and another will write on his hand, the LORD's.

Philippians 3:12-14: Not that I have already obtained this or am already perfect, but I press on to make it my own, because Christ Jesus has made me His own. Brothers, I do not consider that I have made it my own. But one thing I do: forgetting what lies behind and straining forward to what lies ahead. I press on toward the goal for the prize of the upward call of God.

Philippians 3:16: Only let us hold true to what we have attained.

Psalm 66:10: For you, O God, have tested us; you have tried us as silver is tried.

Galatians 5:16-17: So I say, walk by the Spirit, and you will not gratify the desires of the flesh. For the flesh desires what is contrary to the Spirit, and the Spirit what is contrary to the flesh. They are in conflict with each other.

Philippians 4:8-9: Finally, brothers, whatever is true, whatever is honorable, whatever is just, whatever is pure, whatever is lovely, whatever is commendable, if there is any excellence, if there is anything worthy of praise, think about these things. What you have learned and received and heard and seen in me—practice these things, and the God of peace will be with you.

1 Peter 1:4-7: An inheritance that is imperishable, undefiled, and unfading, kept in heaven for you, who by God's power are being guarded through faith for a salvation ready to be revealed in the last time. In this you rejoice, though now for a little while, if necessary, you have been grieved by various trials, so that the tested genuineness of your faith—more precious than gold that perishes though it is tested by fire—may be found to result in praise and glory and honor at the revelation of Jesus Christ.

After a week of this, move into the next class, Hearing His Voice and Resting in Him.

Hearing His Voice
Resting in Him
Class Two

Hearing His Voice

Jesus said, **"My sheep hear My voice" (Matthew 10:27)**. Every Christian I have talked with has a deep desire to hear the voice of the Lord. So how do we do just that?

One of the many ways the Lord communicates with us is in our thoughts, which typically come from three places: our own minds, God, or the enemy.

The Lord flows through our unique personality and places thoughts in our mind that are often light and gentle. But they can be easily disregarded if we aren't aware He can speak to us this way. His thoughts are more loving, kind, peaceful, and full of faith than our ordinary thoughts. They are more positive than ours—wiser, spontaneous, and full of creative ideas that we don't usually think about on our own. Compare these thoughts to those of fear, anxiety, criticalness, anger, or obsessiveness that come from our own thoughts. The Lord's thoughts (placed within our minds) produce peace, joy, excitement, energy, and faith.

Our thoughts can be neutral, or they can be filled with the old, broken patterns of thinking and feeling that we learned from our families growing up. Thoughts and emotions that are filled with fear, anxiety, or depression can be so familiar we often need the Holy Spirit to nudge us so we can **catch ourselves** and take a deeper look at how we are reacting. Finally, the thoughts that are from the enemy are heavy, negative, and critical toward ourselves and others. They are destructive in nature.

> **The thief comes only to steal, kill and destroy. I came that they may have life and have it abundantly. (John 10:10)**

In Soul Breakthrough, we are learning to separate our old ways of thinking from God's thoughts and become more aware, with the help of the Holy Spirit, when we moved into the old patterns of thinking and feeling. As we partner with the Holy Spirit in a new way, by inviting Him to show us areas we are unaware of, or that are so familiar we don't notice they are part of our old man, He enables us to create new pathways in our minds and emotions. This helps us step out of old responses and into our new creation identity- that is full of God and aware of every resource He has given us in heaven.

> **The weapons of our warfare are not of the flesh but have divine power to destroy strongholds. We destroy arguments and every lofty opinion raised against the knowledge of God, and take every thought captive to obey Christ. (2 Corinthians 10:4)**

If you think you don't hear God, don't quit. And please don't compare yourself to anyone else, because the truth is that you are unique, and you hear Him in your own way. Some of you will discover that you have been hearing, seeing, feeling, and receiving knowledge from God for a long time but never realized it was Him. If we ask for the ability to hear, see, feel, and know Him, He will answer us. Look at the two scriptures below.

> **Ask and it will be given to you; seek and you will find; knock and it will be open to you. (Matthew 7:7-11)**

> **Without faith it is impossible to please God, because anyone who comes to Him must believe that He exists and that He rewards those who earnestly seek Him. (Hebrews 11:6)**

Hearing His Voice Saved My Life

It so important that we learn to hear our Lord's voice. I want to share with you how hearing His voice literally saved my life years ago. My husband, my son, who was fifteen at the time, and I decided to take a motorcycle ride from Orange County, California, up to San Francisco. I had learned to ride my own motorcycle while living in Southern California. Our son, Mike, was on the back of the bike my husband, Steve, was riding.

The entire trip took six days. On our way up, we went through the Big Sur area. Let me pause here to tell you that the weather in Northern California is quite different from Southern California. You might have warm air pockets one minute and then suddenly cold, moist areas the next. On a motorcycle, you feel every change in the weather because you are exposed the elements. Northern California weather seemed erratic to me after being accustomed to the mild temperatures in Orange County.

As we continued on our journey north, we rode through a small town in the Big Sur area where construction filled the air with dust. My helmet was already wet from the cold, moist air, and a layer of dust now coated my visor and helmet. Being inexperienced with these weather changes, I was unaware of the effects it would have on my visor.

Adding to this difficulty, the sun was setting and shining directly in my eyes, which made it difficult to see. As I followed my husband, I began to fall behind. Thinking he had continued straight, I continued to ride forward in that direction. **Suddenly I heard in my mind: "Put your visor up now!"** This was God's voice; not mine.

As I put my visor up, I realized we had moved onto a two-lane narrow high way that curved to the right. I had been heading straight and almost *right off a four-hundred-foot cliff*! Swerving abruptly to the right, I moved back into my lane just in time to hear a car honking as it drove straight at me. I immediately moved onto the shoulder and stopped, deeply shaken.

I realized only then that I could not see clearly through my visor because the sun had been in my eyes and the construction dust had covered every inch of the wet helmet. I was so thankful to God that I was able to hear His voice when I did because I would be at the bottom of that four-hundred-foot cliff right now.

This is only one of the many, many times I have heard God, and He has saved me in situations that are both lifesaving and ordinary as well. He is tender toward us and desires a relationship to walk with us moment by moment.

The Many Ways God Speaks

A list of all the ways the Lord communicates with His children would be so long that no book could contain them all. There are millions of creative ways our Lord relates to His children. Because we have each been uniquely created, He chooses to communicate with us in special, personal ways.

However, we can examine the most common ways He communicates with us, His children. One important way is through the Bible. When we read His Word, it transforms our minds and helps us to understand our Lord. The Word renews and washes our minds, bringing them into alignment with His thoughts and ways. When we study the Bible and declare what He has said, faith is deposited within our thoughts and emotions, helping us to understand His ways and His love.

Another form of communication is through prophetic words that we can receive through revelation and then give that message from the Lord to someone else or a group of people. We can also receive prophetic words from those around us that build us up in the Lord. Sometimes, He communicates with us through pictures in our minds. In a gathering at church, I saw an hourglass superimposed on a woman. It was a picture in my mind, and I asked the Lord for more information. He told me that this woman felt as if her time were running out. I saw the Lord turn the hourglass over, giving her more time. I shared this with her, and she agreed that she had been feeling anxious and felt it was too late to do what she wanted in her business. That simple motionless picture in my mind gave her hope and strength that God was taking care of her situation.

Dreams are another amazing way that our Lord speaks to us. Most nights before I go to bed, I ask the Lord to give me a dream from Him. There are even examples in the Old Testament where God spoke to unbelievers in dreams.

Nevertheless, the most common way God speaks to us is with His gentle voice in our own thoughts. Many times, we think it is our own thoughts that we are hearing. If we partner with Him in quieting ourselves from the noise of life and listen, we will discover He is communicating this way quite often.

Resting in Him

Be still before the LORD and wait patiently for Him. (Psalm 37:7)

In returning and rest is your salvation. In quietness and trust your strength. (Isaiah 30:15)

It is important that we learn to quiet ourselves in order to hear His still small voice in our thoughts. Only then, can He fill us with His peace, love, and joy. We all have such busy, hectic lives with little time to rest. Even though it is the Lord who places His thoughts and revelation in our minds, it's our responsibility to quiet ourselves and the noise within us so we can tune in to Him and receive His thoughts. Let's give Him our full, undivided attention!

Radio waves are all around us, but they can only be received if an antenna is "catching" the waves passing by. So too, when we quiet ourselves and believe our Lord is speaking to us, we will catch what He is saying.

I looked up the word **still** in Psalm 46:10 using the Strong's Concordance, a Bible index that includes Hebrew and Greek root words used in the Old and New Testament. In Psalm 46:10 the word *still* in the Strong's Concordance, *raphah*, means "to abate, to cease, to stay, idle, and be still."

Be still and know that I AM GOD. (Psalm 46:10)

Almost thirty years ago, there was a "new move" of the Holy Spirit sweeping across the land. As more and more Christians were filled afresh with the Holy Spirit, the movement spread all over the world and became known as **"the Toronto Blessing"** because it began at the Toronto Airport Vineyard church. The Holy Spirit was released in such a powerful way that people fell to the ground, unable to stand in His presence. I ended up on the ground several times, after encountering the Holy Spirit in these gatherings.

During this season, the Lord began to speak to me about receiving His presence at home, as well. He told me to lie down in my room and rest in Him. So I put a pillow down on my sofa, turned on soft worship music, and felt His presence in an amazing and intimate way.

Resting in the Lord and finding that place of peace in Him is a wonderful way to hear Him speak to us. Honestly, we can face anything if we have deep peace inside. Resting in Him brings healing on the inside as well as the outside. Through the years, I have received enormous healing in areas of emotional brokenness and trauma when I have simply rested with Jesus in my home.

I continue to rest in the Lord this way, receiving His love and strength. Even if we fall asleep while soaking, His Spirit continues to flood us with peace and love.

Blocks or Resistance to Resting in God

Don't be discouraged by the noise or commotion in your thoughts while you rest in the Lord's presence. Recognize that this is part of the journey. We so often want formulas and rules in order to be able to reach the heart of God, but all that is needed is a heart full of determination, faith and a deep desire for His presence.

Spending time with the Lord is similar to tithing—the rewards of peace, joy, hope, and deep intimacy come later. We sow into a wonderful relationship that reaps incredible rewards if we will not get discouraged! It is in these times of resting with the Lord that He tells us who we are and what we are called to do. Right now, beloved, take a minute and quiet yourself.

Enjoy being with Him and receive His peace and love. If thoughts rush in about errands or activities you need to do, just picture pushing them away gently with your hand as you re-focus on the Lord again.

If you have difficulty with your mind wandering, then mediate on scriptures like **"the Kingdom of God is within you" (Luke 17:21).** Or try picturing the scene described in **John 4:4-6:** "He came to a town in Samaria called Sychar... Jacob's well was there, and Jesus, tired as he was from the journey, sat down by the well. It was about noon. When a Samaritan woman came to draw water, Jesus said to her, 'Will you give me a drink?'" Jesus had a conversation with this woman while he was resting. Why don't you rest and talk with Him right now too.

Rest with the Lord for a few minutes. If you receive a thought or picture while being with Him, write it below.

_____

_____

_____

_____

_____

_____

_____

_____

Spend time with the Lord because you are His friend and He enjoys your company. Buy a journal and write down words, scriptures, pictures, songs, or anything else you believe the Lord is saying to you in these moments alone with Him.

Homework: By remembering the teaching and doing the homework each day, you are partnering with the Holy Spirit in transforming areas of your soul that have not been able to change. The Holy Spirit is reprograming those areas of your mind and emotions. Old habits are changing into new ways of thinking. By inviting the Holy Spirit into your day, you are giving Him permission to make you aware of your reactions, while His power and presence is filling your mind and emotions.

Day 1

1. Invite Father God into your day and give the Holy Spirit permission to make you aware when you begin to move into old ways of thinking and feeling in response to familiar triggers. Then breathe deeply and lift your hands and invite Father God to fill you with His presence. Now journal what the Holy Spirit is saying to you.

2. Read several scriptures (feel free to read the scriptures below listed at the end of day seven).

3. Pray in your spiritual language for fifteen minutes or listen to worship music and sing to the Lord for fifteen minutes.

Journal_____

_____

_____

_____

_____

_____

_____

_____

_____

_____

_____

_____

Day 2

1. Invite Father God into your day and give the Holy Spirit permission to make you aware when you begin to move into old ways of thinking and feeling in response to familiar triggers. Then breathe deeply and lift your hands and invite Father God to fill you with His presence. Now journal what the Holy Spirit is saying to you.

2. Read several scriptures (feel free to read the scriptures below listed at the end of day seven).

3. Pray in your spiritual language for fifteen minutes or listen to worship music and sing to the Lord for fifteen minutes.

Journal_____

_____

_____

_____

_____

_____

_____

_____

_____

_____

_____

Day 3

1. Invite Father God into your day and give the Holy Spirit permission to make you aware when you begin to move into old ways of thinking and feeling in response to familiar triggers. Then breathe deeply and lift your hands and invite Father God to fill you with His presence. Now journal what the Holy Spirit is saying to you.

2. Read several scriptures (feel free to read the scriptures below listed at the end of day seven).

3. Pray in your spiritual language for fifteen minutes or listen to worship music and sing to the Lord for fifteen minutes.

Journal_____

_____

_____

_____

_____

_____

_____

_____

_____

_____

_____

_____

_____

_____

Day 4

1. Invite Father God into your day and give the Holy Spirit permission to make you aware when you begin to move into old ways of thinking and feeling in response to familiar

triggers. Then breathe deeply and lift your hands and invite Father God to fill you with His presence. Now journal what the Holy Spirit is saying to you.

2. Read several scriptures (feel free to read the scriptures below listed at the end of day seven).

3. Pray in your spiritual language for fifteen minutes or listen to worship music and sing to the Lord for fifteen minutes.

Journal_____

_____

_____

_____

_____

_____

_____

_____

_____

_____

_____

_____

Day 5

1. Invite Father God into your day and give the Holy Spirit permission to make you aware when you begin to move into old ways of thinking and feeling in response to familiar triggers. Then breathe deeply and lift your hands and invite Father God to fill you with His presence. Now journal what the Holy Spirit is saying to you.

2. Read several scriptures (feel free to read the scriptures below listed at the end of day seven).

3. Pray in your spiritual language for fifteen minutes or listen to worship music and sing to the Lord for fifteen minutes.

Journal_____

_____

_____

_____

_____

_____

_____

_____

_____

_____

_____

Day 6

1. Invite Father God into your day and give the Holy Spirit permission to make you aware when you begin to move into old ways of thinking and feeling in response to familiar triggers. Then breathe deeply and lift your hands and invite Father God to fill you with His presence. Now journal what the Holy Spirit is saying to you.

2. Read several scriptures (feel free to read the scriptures below listed at the end of day seven).

3. Pray in your spiritual language for fifteen minutes or listen to worship music and sing to the Lord for fifteen minutes.

Journal_____

_____

_____

_____

_____

_____

_____

_____

_____

_____

_____

_____

Day 7

1. Invite Father God into your day and give the Holy Spirit permission to make you aware when you begin to move into old ways of thinking and feeling in response to familiar triggers. Then breathe deeply and lift your hands and invite Father God to fill you with His presence. Now journal what the Holy Spirit is saying to you.

2. Read several scriptures (feel free to read the scriptures below listed at the end of day seven).

3. Pray in your spiritual language for fifteen minutes or listen to worship music and sing to the Lord for fifteen minutes.

Journal_____

_____

_____

_____

_____

_____

_____

_____

_____

_____

_____

_____

Daily Scriptures

2 Corinthians 5:17: Therefore if anyone is in Christ, he is a new creation. The old has passed away; behold the new has come.

Jeremiah 29:11: For I know the plans I have for you, declares the Lord, plans to prosper you and not to harm you, plans to give you hope and a future.

Isaiah 26:3: You keep him in perfect peace whose mind is stayed on you, because he trusts in You.

John 10:10: I have come that they may have life and have it to the full.

Exodus 33:14: My Presence will go with you and I will give you rest.

Philippians 4:13: I can do all things through Christ who strengthens me.

Isaiah 41:10: Do not fear, for I am with you; do not be dismayed for I am your God. I will strengthen you and help you; I will uphold you with My righteous right arm.

Proverbs 3:3-6: Trust in the Lord with all your heart, and do not rely on your own understanding. Acknowledge Him in all your ways, and He will make your paths straight.

Romans 8:28: And we know that in all things God works for the good of those who love Him, who have been called according to His purpose.

Matthew 11:29: Come to Me all you who are weary and burdened, and I will give you rest. Take My yoke upon you and learn from Me, for I am gentle and humble in heart and you will find rest for your souls. For My yoke is easy and My burden is light.

Isaiah 44:3-5: I will pour water on the thirsty land, and streams on the dry ground; I will pour out My Spirit on your offspring, and My blessing on your descendants. They shall spring up among the grass like willows by flowing streams. This one will say, 'I am the LORD's...and another will write on his hand, the LORD's.

Philippians 3:12-14: Not that I have already obtained this or am already perfect, but I press on to make it my own, because Christ Jesus has made me His own. Brothers, I do not consider that I have made it my own. But one thing I do: forgetting what lies behind and straining forward to what lies ahead. I press on toward the goal for the prize of the upward call of God in Christ Jesus.

Philippians 3:16: Only let us hold true to what we have attained.

Psalm 66:10: For you, O God, have tested us; you have tried us as silver is tried.

Galatians 5:16-17: So I say, walk by the Spirit, and you will not gratify the desires of the flesh. For the flesh desires what is contrary to the Spirit, and the Spirit what is contrary to the flesh. They are in conflict with each other.

Philippians 4:8-9: Finally, brothers, whatever is true, whatever is honorable, whatever is just, whatever is pure, whatever is lovely, whatever is commendable, if there is any excellence, if there is anything worthy of praise, think about these things. What you have learned and received and heard and seen in me—practice these things, and the God of peace will be with you.

1 Peter 1:4-7: An inheritance that is imperishable, undefiled, and unfading, kept in heaven for you, who by God's power are being guarded through faith for a salvation ready to be revealed in the last time. In this you rejoice, though now for a little while, if necessary, you have been grieved by various trials, so that the tested genuineness of your faith—more precious than gold that perishes though it is tested by fire—may be found to result in praise and glory and honor at the revelation of Jesus Christ.

After a week, move to the next class The Refining Process with God, Understanding His Ways.

God's Refining Process
Understanding His Ways
Class Three

Many Christians have been shipwrecked in their faith because they did not understand the ways of God. Then when difficulty came, they thought God was angry with them, or they assumed He should have been like Santa Claus. These Christians were unaware of the refining process we walk through with God.

God the Father wants a relationship with each one of us that has such a level of trust and friendship that when difficulty and trials come, we don't lose faith, and we continue to recognize His loving character.

Knowing my Father this way has helped me stand through some of the most difficult trials, including childhood sexual abuse. He helped me to see the trials in my life through His perspective, and He has brought enormous healing on the inside as well as physical healing.

Several years ago, when God asked me to partner with Him in releasing the Soul Breakthrough teaching, He handed me a solid gold rose, in a vision, and said this represented the Soul Breakthrough classes and what I was called to teach, equip, and give to other Christians.

> **But He knows the way that I take; when He has tried me, I shall come out as gold. (Job 23:10)**

> **I will put this third into the fire, and refine them as one refines silver, and test them as gold is tested. They will call upon My name, and I will answer them. I will say, they are My people; they will say, the LORD is my God. (Zechariah 13:9)**

Roses are delicate and fragrant. They express promise, hope, and a new beginning. Have you ever heard the phrase, "You will come out smelling like a rose?" That means to have success in a situation in which one was likely to fail or be harmed. Everything will turn out alright. (Remember the movie *The Blue Rose*? The rose was used to bring instant healing.) One interesting play on words, the word *rose* also means "to stand or to rise up," which is what Soul Breakthrough is all about, rising up and standing in who we are and what He has done.

In the Bible, **gold** represents holiness, purity, and glory. Gold is a precious metal of great value, and it is highly desired. It's associated with that which is holy to God and is used to describe the precious nature of His Word and Law:

> **The judgments of the Lord are true and righteous altogether. More to be desired are they then gold, yea, then much fine gold. (Psalm 19:9-10)**

Can you see how a solid gold rose would represent perfectly the teaching of Soul Breakthrough? Roses are beautiful but fragile. The golden rose the Lord showed me represents the same beauty but with the strength of the Lord. God is giving us His Spirit moment by moment throughout our day to fill the fragile, broken, old nature and transform it into promise, hope, and a new beginning. As we practice His presence each day and invite Him into the old fears and broken ways, then we rise up and stand in who He has created us to be and move into the new creation.

Here is an example of how our loving God transforms areas in us full of trauma and brokenness into His beauty, life, and love. When I was twelve years old, our family moved back to the United States from England. During our stay in England, I had experienced several traumatic experiences involving sexual abuse that left me in shock and deeply broken. This had happened numerous times before we moved to England, but these new traumatic experiences were more severe and terrified me.

Moving back to California, my father took us to our new home, which was huge and beautiful. My older sister received a lovely room with a balcony overlooking the rose garden, and she and my older brother had their own bathrooms attached to their rooms. My three younger brothers were shown an enormous room, three times the size of a normal one, to share between them.

I waited in anticipation for my room, but it never came. It appeared that they had forgotten me, and there were no more rooms! I was in a very vulnerable place because of the trauma in England, and I immediately felt all the familiar feelings of being overlooked, discounted, rejected, dishonored, and insignificant. Finally, my mom had an idea and took me to a small room that had once served as a powder room with a small bathroom. She lovingly and painstakingly transformed it into a precious room just for me.

My room was halfway up the stairs, which made me feel half as valuable as everyone else. As I gazed up at the landing where the rest of my family lived, I felt overwhelmed by feelings of deep emotional pain, lack of safety, worthlessness, insignificance, and damage when compared with my brothers and sister.

Had I not been so injured by the experiences in England, I would have been ecstatic to receive my own room. But because of the sexual abuse throughout my childhood, especially in England, I wasn't able to respond to this experience in a healthy manner.

I have received tremendous healing from the Lord over the issue of feeling valuable, safe, and loved. As with many of us, my injuries continued through my life to be repeated over and over again, but Jesus stepped in each time, like a Master healer, and gave me a choice to forgive and come to him to receive healing, safety, and value.

Recently, the Lord took me back to that little room halfway up the stairs and told me it had been a gift from him all along. He said, "**Change the way you look at this.**" As he said this, I saw a vision of Him sitting on my bed in that little room, but this time He was surrounded by deep, rich, elegance. I looked around at the walls embedded with jewels, the furnishings like something from a palace, and small vats of warm oil scattered around my room. He told me He'd been the one who had blessed me with my own room because it had been there that He had filled me with His Spirit and begun a journey of healing and deep intimacy with me. I realize now that God allowed that painful experience, and all the others, so I would become who I am today. My deep need for Him was only accentuated by those experiences.

When we find ourselves in the throes of painful experiences or memories of them, He will be there with us. And if we partner with our Lord, the trauma and pain we experience will become a place of transformation and beauty when He moves into it. (I found out years later, as an adult, that my parents had miscounted the rooms and thought there had been another room next to my sister's for me.)

When we feel unloved, over-looked, unnoticed, or discounted and we have other injuries from parents or authority figures, this can leave deep wounds and gaping holes in our hearts. We start to compare ourselves with those around us and we feel envy, jealousy, bitterness, and self-pity. Then emotional pain and noise creeps in between us and our Beloved, making it harder to hear His voice clearly.

Let us allow Him to heal the pain that caused these injuries. Then our hearts can rest again in Him and listen to His words of love and comfort. Beloved, let's invite the Holy Spirit into those memories to flood them with His presence, bringing His healing into our broken souls.

The Silversmith

There is a true story I read on the internet about a silversmith that touched my heart. A group of women were studying the book of Malachi and came across this verse in chapter 3, **"He will sit as a refiner and purifier of silver" (Malachi 3:3).** They were puzzled, wondering what the scripture meant about the character of God.

One of the women offered to find out about the process of refining silver and get back to the group at their next Bible study. That week she contacted a silversmith and made an appointment to watch him at work. She didn't mention anything about the reason for her interest in silver beyond her curiosity about the process of refining silver. As she watched, the silversmith held a piece of silver over the fire and let it heat up. He explained that, in refining silver, one needed to hold the silver in the middle of the fire where the flames were hottest to burn away all the impurities.

The woman thought about God holding us in such a hot spot. Then she thought again about the verse, that He sits as a refiner and purifier of silver. Asking the silversmith if it was true that he had to sit there in front of the fire the whole time the silver was being refined, he replied yes. Not only did he sit there holding the silver, but furthermore he kept his eyes on the silver the entire time it was in the fire. The woman was silent for a moment. Then she asked the silversmith, "How do you know when the silver is fully refined?" He smiled at her and answered, "Oh, that's the easy part, **when I see my image reflected in it."**

In both the Old and New Testaments, we find numerous references to the refining of gold and silver as a parallel of God's refining us through painful trials. This metaphor helps us understand the Lord's purpose—to conform us to the character

56

of Christ. Character is forged over time, especially through fiery trials. Indeed, God is our refiner.

For you, God, tested us, You refined us as silver. (Psalm 66:10)

An inheritance that is imperishable, undefiled, and unfading, kept in heaven for you, who by God's power are being guarded through faith for a salvation ready to be revealed in the last time. In this you rejoice, though now for a little while, if necessary, you have been grieved by various trials, so that the tested genuineness of your faith—more precious than gold that perishes though it is tested by fire—may be found to result in praise and glory and honor at the revelation of Jesus Christ. (1 Peter 1:4-7)

Two Hebrew words have been translated *refine*: **tsaraph**—"to fuse, melt, purge"; and **zaqaq;**—"to strain or sift." In the case of silver and gold, the term probably referred to some washing process in connection with refining. Can you see how God washes us, sifts us, and refines us in His wonderful process of love?

Metallurgy

Metallurgy is the science of preparing metals, such as gold or silver, for use by separating them from their ores and purifying them to extract the valuable element or elements. This process removes the impurities from the metals.

In biblical times, a refiner began by breaking up rough, hardened rock. That rock might have rare metals hidden within—the precious metals of gold and silver. The breaking of the rock was necessary to begin the refining process to expose highly valuable metals to heat.

Then the crushed rock was placed into a fireproof melting pot able to withstand extreme heat. The furnace was at a temperature necessary for removing other metals that would ruin the quality of the gold or silver. Just as the furnace was used to purify silver and gold, so the Lord uses heat to cleanse our hearts.

> **The crucible for silver and the furnace for gold, but the Lord tests the heart. (Proverbs 17:3)**

As the rock melted, a layer of impurities called *dross* formed on the surface. For us personally, dross represents anything that keeps us from the Lord and being all that He wants us to be. The Bible says, **"Remove the dross from the silver, and a silversmith can produce a vessel" Proverbs 25:4.**

After skimming off these impurities, the heat was turned up and the rock placed back into the furnace. Again and again, up to seven times, impurities rose to the surface. Each time impurities are removed, they leave behind refined gold and silver.

> **He knows the way that I take; when He has tested me, I will come forth as gold. (Job 23:10)**

As we trust the Lord to use our trials to cleanse our character and purify our hearts, we will begin to see how loving our God truly is and trust His hand in our life.

Remember: the pain God allows in your life has purpose. The heat is never intended to destroy you, only to conform you into the character of Christ. As the heat of painful circumstances intensifies in your life, know that the Lord will never leave you or forsake you.

He will sit as a refiner and purifier of silver; He will purify . . . and refine them like gold and silver. (Malachi 3:3)

Sit with the Lord for a minute. Ask Him to show you a painful situations in your past. Now invite the Holy Spirit to show you that situation through God's eyes. The Lord will help you to forgive those who injured you. The words of Jesus echo through the generations as He hung on the cross.

Father, forgive them, for they know not what they do. (John 23:34)

Ask Him how He has used, is using, and will use that trauma or circumstance for good in your life.

And we know that all things work together for good to them that love God, to them who are called according to His purpose. (Romans 8:28)

Write down what He reveals to you and what He shows you.

_____

_____

_____

_____

_____

_____

_____

_____

Homework:

Day 1

1. Invite Father God into your day and give the Holy Spirit permission to make you aware when you begin to move into old ways of thinking and feeling in response to familiar triggers. Then breathe deeply and lift your hands and invite Father God to fill you with His presence. Now journal what the Holy Spirit is saying to you.

2. Read several scriptures (feel free to read the scriptures below listed at the end of day seven).

3. Pray in your spiritual language for fifteen minutes or listen to worship music and sing to the Lord for fifteen minutes.

Journal_____

_____

_____

_____

_____

_____

_____

_____

_____

_____

_____

_____

Day 2

1. Invite Father God into your day and give the Holy Spirit permission to make you aware when you begin to move into old ways of thinking and feeling in response to familiar triggers. Then breathe deeply and lift your hands and invite Father God to fill you with His presence. Now journal what the Holy Spirit is saying to you.

2. Read several scriptures (feel free to read the scriptures below listed at the end of day seven).

3. Pray in your spiritual language for fifteen minutes or listen to worship music and sing to the Lord for fifteen minutes.

Journal_____

_____

_____

_____

_____

_____

_____

_____

_____

_____

_____

_____

_____

Day 3

1. Invite Father God into your day and give the Holy Spirit permission to make you aware when you begin to move into old ways of thinking and feeling in response to familiar triggers. Then breathe deeply and lift your hands and invite Father God to fill you with His presence. Now journal what the Holy Spirit is saying to you.

2. Read several scriptures (feel free to read the scriptures below listed at the end of day seven).

3. Pray in your spiritual language for fifteen minutes or listen to worship music and sing to the Lord for fifteen minutes.

Journal_____

_____

_____

_____

_____

_____

_____

_____

_____

_____

_____

Day 4

1. Invite Father God into your day and give the Holy Spirit permission to make you aware when you begin to move into old ways of thinking and feeling in response to familiar triggers. Then breathe deeply and lift your hands and invite Father God to fill you with His presence. Now journal what the Holy Spirit is saying to you.

2. Read several scriptures (feel free to read the scriptures below listed at the end of day seven).

3. Pray in your spiritual language for fifteen minutes or listen to worship music and sing to the Lord for fifteen minutes.

Journal_____

_____

_____

_____

_____

_____

_____

_____

_____

_____

_____

Day 5

1. Invite Father God into your day and give the Holy Spirit permission to make you aware when you begin to move into old ways of thinking and feeling in response to familiar triggers. Then breathe deeply and lift your hands and invite

Father God to fill you with His presence. Now journal what the Holy Spirit is saying to you.

2. Read several scriptures (feel free to read the scriptures below listed at the end of day seven).

3. Pray in your spiritual language for fifteen minutes or listen to worship music and sing to the Lord for fifteen minutes.

Journal_____

_____

_____

_____

_____

_____

_____

_____

_____

_____

_____

Day 6

1. Invite Father God into your day and give the Holy Spirit permission to make you aware when you begin to move into old ways of thinking and feeling in response to familiar triggers. Then breathe deeply and lift your hands and invite Father God to fill you with His presence. Now journal what the Holy Spirit is saying to you.

2. Read several scriptures (feel free to read the scriptures below listed at the end of day seven).

3. Pray in your spiritual language for fifteen minutes or listen to worship music and sing to the Lord for fifteen minutes.

Journal_____

_____

_____

_____

_____

_____

_____

_____

_____

_____

Day 7

1. Invite Father God into your day and give the Holy Spirit permission to make you aware when you begin to move into old ways of thinking and feeling in response to familiar triggers. Then breathe deeply and lift your hands and invite Father God to fill you with His presence. Now journal what the Holy Spirit is saying to you.

2. Read several scriptures (feel free to read the scriptures below listed at the end of day seven).

3. Pray in your spiritual language for fifteen minutes or listen to worship music and sing to the Lord for fifteen minutes.

Journal_____

_____

_____

_____

_____

_____

_____

_____

_____

_____

_____

_____

Daily Scriptures

2 Corinthians 5:17: Therefore if anyone is in Christ, he is a new creation. The old has passed away; behold the new has come.

Jeremiah 29:11: For I know the plans I have for you, declares the Lord, plans to prosper you and not to harm you, plans to give you hope and a future.

Isaiah 26:3: You keep him in perfect peace whose mind is stayed on you, because he trusts in You.

John 10:10: I have come that they may have life and have it to the full.

Exodus 33:14: My Presence will go with you and I will give you rest.

Philippians 4:13: I can do all things through Christ who strengthens me.

Isaiah 41:10: Do not fear, for I am with you; do not be dismayed for I am your God. I will strengthen you and help you; I will uphold you with My righteous right arm.

Proverbs 3:3-6: Trust in the Lord with all your heart, and do not rely on your own understanding. Acknowledge Him in all your ways, and He will make your paths straight.

Romans 8:28: And we know that in all things God works for the good of those who love Him, who have been called according to His purpose.

Matthew 11:29: Come to Me all you who are weary and burdened, and I will give you rest. Take My yoke upon you and learn from Me, for I am gentle and humble in heart and you will find rest for your souls. For My yoke is easy and My burden is light.

Isaiah 44:3-5: I will pour water on the thirsty land, and streams on the dry ground; I will pour out My Spirit on your offspring, and My blessing on your descendants. They shall spring up among the grass like willows by flowing streams. This one will say, 'I am the LORD's...and another will write on his hand, the LORD's.

Philippians 3:12-14: Not that I have already obtained this or am already perfect, but I press on to make it my own, because Christ Jesus has made me His own. Brothers, I do not consider that I have made it my own. But one thing I do: forgetting what lies behind and straining forward to what lies ahead. I press on toward the goal for the prize of the upward call of God in Christ Jesus.

Philippians 3:16: Only let us hold true to what we have attained.

Psalm 66:10: For you, O God, have tested us; you have tried us as silver is tried.

Galatians 5:16-17: So I say, walk by the Spirit, and you will not gratify the desires of the flesh. For the flesh desires what is contrary to the Spirit, and the Spirit what is contrary to the flesh. They are in conflict with each other.

Philippians 4:8-9: Finally, brothers, whatever is true, whatever is honorable, whatever is just, whatever is pure, whatever is lovely, whatever is commendable, if there is any excellence, if there is anything worthy of praise, think about these things. What you have learned and received and heard and seen in me—practice these things, and the God of peace will be with you.

1 Peter 1:4-7: An inheritance that is imperishable, undefiled, and unfading, kept in heaven for you, who by God's power are being guarded through faith for a salvation ready to be revealed in the last time. In this you rejoice, though now for a little while, if necessary, you have been grieved by various trials, so that the tested genuineness of your faith—more precious than gold that perishes though it is tested by fire—may be found to result in praise and glory and honor at the revelation of Jesus Christ.

After a week, move to the next class, Risk, Walking into Your Promised Land.

RISK

Walking into the Promised Land
Class Four

We are now entering the fourth week of Soul Breakthrough and the final lap of our race, so let's review our first three weeks. Hopefully, you have been able to do the homework daily. The importance of this cannot be stressed. The Holy Spirit, through repetition, is creating a new track in your thoughts and emotions and breaking the old habits.

Soul Breakthrough is about standing in the new creation that we are now and walking with the Lord into our Promised Land.

Let's review the first three weeks so we can reinforce the Soul Breakthrough process.

The First Week.

Remember the vision I shared. I saw myself running in a race with a large group of people who were very close to the finish line of this season. The Lord was beside us, encouraging us to run through the finish line. However, the enemy had set up smoke and mirrors that completely covered the finish line so we could not see it; it was hidden.

Jesus wants us, by faith, to run right through the smoke and mirrors, into the new season He has for each of us. Beloved, we are so much closer to moving into this new and amazing season than the enemy wants us to believe. Jesus is offering to transform our minds and emotions so we can move into His healing and His new nature.

Many of us have had years of sermons, worship, prayer, healing, counseling, and God pouring into our lives.

Do you remember the broken leg analog? I asked you to imagine that your leg was broken and the Lord sovereignly healed it. But, out of habit, you continued to limp around, forgetting that your leg had been restored. This is how we often walk in our daily lives. When a crisis occurs, we tend to forget all the wonderful things the Lord has done for us and all the areas in our lives He has healed. We forget that we are new creations in Him, filled with His Spirit, having access to every resource available in heaven.

Beloved, these last three weeks you chose to stand in your healing by inviting the Father to fill you every day. You invited the Holy Spirit to immediately move into those thoughts and emotions not allowing old habits of thinking or feeling to move you back into your old nature. Now it's time to step fully into who you are called to be, walking moment-by-moment with His Spirit.

> **Therefore if anyone is in Christ, he is a new creation. The old has passed away; behold the new has come. (2 Corinthians 5:17)**

> **One thing I do: forgetting what lies behind and straining forward to what lies ahead, I press on towards the goal for the prize of the upward call of God in Christ Jesus. Let those of us who are mature think this way, and if in anything you think otherwise, God will reveal that also to you. Only let us hold true to what we have attained. (Philippians 3:12-16)**

You developed an awareness of the Holy Spirit each morning and during the day. When you went back into the old ways of thinking and feeling, you lifted your hands and invited the Lord to fill you with His Spirit. You have been realigning your mind with God's mind, your thoughts with His thoughts. Repetition has change the pathways in your brain and created new corridors of thinking.

The key is changing our thinking from the old to the new by inviting His presence to fill us.

The Second Week

In the second week, we looked at some of the ways the Lord communicates with us. He said, **"My sheep hear My Voice"** **(John 10:27).** That means every one of us that knows Jesus can hear Him.

Our thoughts come from three places: our heart, God, or the enemy, just like dreams. With the help of the Holy Spirit, we learn to rightly divide the thoughts He places in our minds from our own thoughts and the enemy's.

It is essential that we learn to recognize His Voice in our thoughts, this is the most common way He speaks to us.

> **For the weapons of our warfare are not of the flesh but have divine power to destroy strongholds. We destroy arguments and every lofty opinion raised against the knowledge of God, and take every thought captive to obey Christ. (2 Corinthians 10:4)**

His thoughts inside our mind are more loving, kind, peaceful, and full of faith than our normal thoughts. They cause peace, excitement, energy, and faith. God's thoughts are lighter than our thoughts. The content of the thoughts are wiser, more loving, and they have concepts or ideas that we don't usually think. His thoughts are spontaneous. Our own thoughts can be neutral or filled with the old ways of thinking and feeling. The enemy's thoughts are heavier and will be critical of us and others and destructive in nature.

As we learn to quiet ourselves, we can distinguish His voice in our thoughts from the other thoughts and noise.

Be still and know that I am God. (Psalm 46:10)

I looked up the word **still** in Psalm 46:10 using the Strong's Concordance, a Bible index that includes Hebrew and Greek root words used in the Old and New Testament. In Psalm 46:10 the word *still* in the Strong's Concordance, *raphah*, means "to abate, to cease, to stay, idle, and be still."

Resting in the Lord and finding that place of peace in Him is a wonderful way to hear Him speak to us. Honestly, we can face anything if we have deep peace inside. *Resting* with Him brings healing on the inside as well as the outside.

What we are doing in Soul Breakthrough, partnering with the Holy Spirit, is noticing the difference between our thoughts and God's thoughts in our mind. The apostle Paul urges us in the Bible to walk by the Spirit and not in our old nature.

> **So I say, walk by the Spirit, and you will not gratify the desires of the flesh. For the flesh desires what is contrary to the Spirit, and the Spirit what is contrary to the flesh. They are in conflict with each other. (Galatians 5:16-17)**

> **Put off your old self, which belongs to your former manner of life and is corrupt through deceitful desires, and be renewed in the spirit of your minds, and put on your new self, created after the likeness of God in true righteousness and holiness. (Ephesians 4:22)**

The Third Week

The third week, we looked at the ways God refines us, enabling us to become more like Him and have deeper, fuller relationships with Him. Many Christians don't understand His ways, and when difficulty comes, they think God is angry with them or punishing them. But God loves us and wants a relationship with us that helps us to stand through our most difficult trials, knowing He loves us.

In the Bible, there are examples of the process that gold and silver go through, using severe heat to remove the impurities in these metals. A refiner began by breaking up rough, hardened rock that had the precious metals of gold and silver. The breaking of the rock was necessary to begin the refining process to expose highly valuable metals to heat.

Then the crushed rock was placed into a fireproof melting pot at a temperature necessary for removing other metals that would ruin the quality of the gold or silver. Just as the furnace was used to purify silver and gold, so the Lord uses heat to cleanse our hearts.

> **The crucible for silver, the furnace for gold, but the
> Lord tests the heart. (Proverbs 17:3)**

As the rock melted, impurities called *dross* formed on the surface. For us personally, dross represents anything that keeps us from the Lord and being all that He wants us to be. The Bible says,

> **Remove the dross from the silver, and a silversmith
> can produce a vessel. (Proverbs 25:4)**

After skimming off these impurities, the heat was turned up and the rock placed back into the furnace. Again and again, impurities rose to the surface.

> **He knows the way I take; when He has tested me, I will come forth as gold. (Job 23:10)**

As we trust the Lord to use our trials to cleanse our character and purify our hearts, we will begin to see how loving our God truly is and trust His hand in our lives.

Remember: the pain God allows in your life has purpose—to conform you into the character of Christ. As the heat of painful circumstances intensifies, know that the Lord will never leave you or forsake you.

> **He will sit as a refiner and purifier of silver; he will purify...and refine them like gold and silver. (Malachi 3:3)**

The Lord helps you to see pain and trauma differently—through His eyes. He has and will use that trauma or painful circumstance for good in your life.

Risk
Walking into the Promised Land
Class Four

Soul Breakthrough is about standing in the new creation that we are now and walking with the Lord into our Promised Land.

Father God wants us to take **risks**. It's time to move forward and think with His thoughts. We need to **risk** and move into the Promised Land the Lord has for each of us. When we know we are new creations then we are able to **risk**. When we are ruled by heaven, we will take risks for His sake.

What do I mean by **risk**? Stepping out to share Jesus with someone in a store. Doing something we have thought about but never step into: writing a book, teaching a class, leading a worship song, learning to play an instrument, going back to school. The list is as creative as you are. Ask the Holy Spirit what He wants you to step into and where He wants you to **risk**.

Israel in the Wilderness Forty Years – Stuck in the Old Way of Thinking

Let's look at the children of Israel before they moved into their Promised Land. We can learn much from them about trusting God and choosing faith and not fear.

The Lord had promised Moses that Israel would possess a land flowing with milk and honey and that the Lord would make the people successful in driving out the inhabitants of that land.

> **And you shall take possession of the land and settle in it, for I have given you the land to possess. (Numbers 33:53)**

After the flight from Egypt, the Lord led Israel through the wilderness until they reached the land He had promised to give them. He said to Moses,

> **Send some men to explore the land of Canaan, which I am giving to the Israelites. (Numbers 13:2)**

So when Israel arrived at the border of the Promised Land of Canaan, Moses sent twelve spies to scout out the land as a future home for the Israelite people. At the end of forty days, the spies brought back a report for the whole community and showed them the fruit of the land. One branch with a single cluster of grapes had to be carried out of the land by two men.

> **We went into the land to which you sent us, and it does flow with milk and honey, here is its fruit. But the people who live there are strong, and the cities are fortified and very large...We can't attack those people; they are stronger than we are! (Numbers 13:27-31)**

Israel became convinced they could not get rid of the current people in the land, even though **God had told them they could.** Because ten of the scouts report about the land was negative, a mood of deep depression overwhelmed Israel.

But there were two scouts who disagreed, Caleb and Joshua: "We must go up and take possession of the land." Only Joshua and Caleb stood up and said it was a good land.

> **The land we passed through and explored is exceedingly good. If the LORD is pleased with us, He will lead us into that land, a land flowing with milk and honey, and will give it to us. Only do not rebel against the LORD, and do not be afraid of the people of the land...Their protection is gone, but the LORD is with us. (Numbers 14:7-9)**

The whole community threatened to stone them, but then the glory of the Lord appeared, and the Lord responded.

> **None of the men who have seen My glory and My signs that I did in Egypt and in the wilderness ...shall see the land I swore to give their**

fathers...But My servant Caleb, because he has a different spirit and has followed Me fully, I will bring into the land into which he went, and his descendants shall possess it. (Numbers 14:22-24)

As a result, the entire nation was made to wander in the desert for forty years, until almost the whole generation of men had died. Joshua and Caleb (the two spies who brought back a good report and believed that God would help them succeed) were the only men from their generation permitted to go into the Promised Land after the forty years.

God told them that all of the men who were twenty years and older would not enter into the Promised Land due to **their lack of faith and belief in Him**. They would all wander in the desert for forty years until they had died. But Joshua and Caleb and the younger generation under twenty years of age would go into the Promised Land.

Israel had a problem with their imagination—their thoughts were filled with fear and insecurity rather than faith. God wanted to train Israel's minds so they could see the blessings and opportunities He was offering them in the Promised Land.

Joshua Enters the Promised Land

Forty years of wandering in the wilderness brought Israel to a mountaintop overlooking the land of promise. God now told Joshua not to fear or be afraid but to go and take possession of the Promised Land. Every Israelite over twenty years of age when they'd left Egypt under Moses's leadership was now dead, except for three people: Moses, Joshua, and Caleb (Numbers 14:38).

When God spoke to Joshua, He did not talk about the enemies waiting for them in the Promised Land but two enemies they would face that could actually keep them from His promise. The biggest enemies Israel faced were discouragement and fear, not armies or giants in the land. Faith in what God had promised was what was most needed, not fear.

> **Have I not commanded you? Be strong and courageous. Do not be afraid; do not be discouraged, for the LORD your God will be with you wherever you go. (Joshua 1:9)**

God's words to Joshua are the same words He gives to us. The only way to fight fear and discouragement is to be strong and courageous, to take hold of His Word, believe, and obey it. Beloved, lets believe what the Lord has said in His Word and let Him transform our thoughts and emotions. It is time to take a risk, a leap of faith.

God Wants Us to Enter Our Promised Land

We can look at the children of Israel and learn from them. It is obvious God wants us to have faith to believe He will do what He said. He has good things for us and wants to bless His children, but we need to partner with Him in changing our thoughts and emotions, replacing fear with faith in Him.

> **For I know the plans I have for you, declares the LORD, plans for welfare and not for evil, to give you a future and a hope. (Jeremiah 19:11)**

Referring to Israel's wilderness experience, the apostle Paul wrote, "**These things happened to them as examples and were** written down as warnings for us, on whom the fulfillment of the ages has come" (1 Corinthians 10:11).

Joshua and Caleb were able to go into the Promised Land because they **wholeheartedly followed God.** They had full faith in God that He could do what He said, defeat all of their enemies once they went into the Promised Land to conquer and possess it. They believed His word and obeyed His word. Look what the Lord did for them because of their faith.

> **The LORD gave them rest on every side just as He had sworn to their fathers. Not one of all their enemies had withstood them, for the LORD had given all their enemies into their hands. Not one word of all the good promises that the LORD had made to the house of Israel failed. All came to pass. (Joshua 21:44–45)**

Like Israel in the wilderness, you and I are between promise and fulfillment. Like the Israelites in the wilderness, we have been delivered from captivity, but we have not reached our final destination and resting place yet. Even in our Promised Land, we will continue to work out, by faith, the promises the Lord has spoken to us. The apostle Paul explains this so many years ago.

> **Not that I have already obtained all this, or have already arrived at my goal, but I press on to take hold of that for which Christ Jesus took hold of me. Brothers and sisters, I do not consider myself yet to have taken hold of it. But one thing I do: Forgetting what is behind and straining toward what is ahead, I press on toward the goal to win the prize for which God has called me heavenward in Christ Jesus. (Philippians 3:12-14)**

Many people enter their Promised Land, but because of trials and difficulties, they think they have moved back into the wilderness. Not so. It is the attitude in our hearts that allows us to remain in our Promised Land with the Lord. And when we move back into the old ways of thinking and feeling, now, we can invite the Lord into our thoughts to transform them and stay in our Promised Land

As you progressed through the Soul Breakthrough workbook, I know that the Spirit showed you something in your life that He was partnering with you in transforming. It was probably difficult the first week because you were in the habit of thinking and feeling the old ways in that area. But now a new pathway is developing in your brain through the Holy Spirit. No longer do you need to react in the old ways, but now you can choose to walk by the Spirit in that area.

Our Promised Land

Our Promised Land is any area in our life that we are walking by the Holy Spirit and in the new creation God birthed in us when we accepted His Son as our Savior and Lord.

Our Promised Land is walking in peace and intimacy with God throughout the day, responding with the Holy Spirit and not reacting when difficulty comes our way, inviting the Father to fill us when we begin to move back to old habits.

Our Promised Land is also moving forward in boldness to be who God called us to be. One synonym for the word *risk* is *adventure,* and the opposite is safety. If you remember, Israel had to go and take their Promise Land. They had to fight their enemies, but the Lord was with them and told them they would succeed.

Israel, with Joshua, stepped boldly into the Promised Land, knowing it was full of hostile people groups. They chose to believe God when He said He would defeat their enemies. The words Father God spoke to Joshua right before they began to cross over the Jordan into the land full of milk and honey was to be strong and courageous.

> **Be strong and courageous. Do not be frightened and do not be dismayed, for the LORD your God is with you wherever you go. (Joshua 1:9)**

The Lord wants us to risk or go on an adventure with him, not playing it safe anymore. He reminds us that He will go with us and give us rest. Does this mean we will not have trials? It means **when** we have trails and difficult situations, He will be with us and fill us with His perspective, power, and love to respond differently and see the circumstances from His eyes.

> **And we know that for those who love God all things work together for good, for those who are called according to His purpose. (Romans 8:28)**

Beloved, it is time now to believe what the Lord is saying in the Bible to us. To take those words personally and apply them to our lives. To choose faith and not fear, knowing our God is also our friend. He tells us throughout the Bible not to fear because He will never leave or forsake us.

We are now going to walk boldly with the Lord, out of the wilderness, through the Jordan River and into our Promised Land. This is a prophetic act of faith.

Sit quietly with the Lord and, by faith, picture yourself

walking across the Jordan into your Promised Land, hand in hand with Jesus.

You can stand up and say this or even walk forward as you proclaim this.

Now speak out loud, "I am now moving out of my wilderness into a new season and into my Promised Land. The Lord will walk with me and never leave me. He will help me to be successful in defeating my enemies."

Leaders Guide
Chapter Five

Soul Breakthrough is suitable for individual, group, or church participation. Then each child of God walks it out on their own during the week until the group meets again.

It is in these communities that this course has the most effect. My desire and pray is that God partners with you to release breakthrough in the people He has given you.

Gather those interested in your group or church once a week for four weeks. Each week, there will be daily homework as they learn to walk by the Spirit throughout the day.

Homework is essential! The Holy Spirit is partnering with each person during the week to produce change in their lives. When they invite Him into the daily moment-by-moment circumstances, and give Him permission to make them aware of how they are reacting, old patterns and ways of thinking are disrupted, and a new track begins to form in their mind and emotions. If they do this every day for several weeks, then new ways of thinking and feeling are created by the Holy Spirit.

The apostle Paul said to **"walk by the Spirit" (Galatians 5:16**.) The Creator of all things wants to fill us with new life, new ways of thinking, and new ways of seeing and feeling.

Preparing for Soul Breakthrough

Worship Leader or CD

Find someone to lead worship for the four weeks of this course, or you can listen to a CD and worship the Lord that way. Soaking CDs are good as they quiet the people and focus them on the Lord.

When doing Soul Breakthrough as a group, the last class will not have a discussion time or homework like the first three classes. It will need worship music or a worship leader to play while the people symbolically walk through the Jordan (a tunnel made up of the team leaders) into their Promised Land.

Video

For the group sessions there will be a short teaching video for each of the four classes around twenty-to-twenty-five minutes. This video will cover that week's teaching. Watch this together before breaking into small groups (if your group is large).

Team Leaders

If your group is large, invite mature people in your community or church to lead small groups for the discussion time. Try to keep the small groups at twelve people or less, which creates a more intimate setting for people to share. People are more comfortable to open up in a group of twelve or less. Set up tables for each leader to gather with his or her small group.

There will be a discussion question for each of the first three classes.

Group Sessions:

Worship

Open with worship for half an hour and then share this scripture in the large group,

> **Therefore, if anyone is in Christ, he is a new creation. The old has passed away; behold, the new has come. (2 Corinthians 5:17)**

Pray over your time together that God the Father will do far more than you ask or think.

Small Group Discussion

Now bring your team leaders to the front and introduce them so the group can see them. As the leader moves to the table or area where they will be doing the discussion, tell everyone to pick a group. You can go around and ask people in larger groups to move to smaller ones in order for the groups to be around the same size. Anywhere from three to twelve people per group is good but no larger than twelve people because the feeling of intimacy and community is difficult to create with more people than twelve.

Reminder to Do the Homework

It is crucial that the small group leaders reminds their people to follow the homework each day until you meet again the following week. This way, those taking this course partner with God during their day and move into a deeper, more intimate relationship with Him. No teaching, ministry, or person can replace their relationship with the living God and His impact on their daily lives.

The homework is below.

1. Invite Father God into your day and give the Holy Spirit permission to make you aware when you begin to move into old ways of thinking and feeling in response to familiar triggers. Then breathe deeply and lift your hands and invite

Father God to fill you with His presence. Now journal what the Holy Spirit is saying to you.

2. Read several scriptures (feel free to read the scriptures below listed at the end of day seven).

3. Pray in your spiritual language for fifteen minutes. If your group does not have a spiritual language (the gift of tongues), then tell them to listen to worship music and sing to the Lord for fifteen minutes.

For those of you not sure what "praying in your spiritual language" means, I am referring to one of the nine gifts of the Holy Spirit, the gift of tongues, shown below:

> When the day of Pentecost arrived, they were all together in one place. And suddenly there came from heaven a sound like a mighty rushing wind, and it filled the entire house where they were sitting. And divided tongues as of fire appeared to them and rested on each one of them. And they were all filled with the Holy Spirit and began to speak in other tongues as the Spirit gave them utterance. (Acts 2:1-4)

> I thank God that I speak in tongues more than all of you._Nevertheless, in church I would rather speak five words with my mind in order to instruct others, than ten thousand words in a tongue. (1 Corinthian 14:18-19)

> Anyone who speaks in a tongue edifies themselves, but the one who prophesies edifies the church. (1 Corinthians 14:4)

A few more scriptures on this for further study are Acts 19:6, 1 Corinthians 12:8-10, and 1 Corinthians 12:4, 21, 22.

Soul Breakthrough
Class One
Our Broken Soul Transformed by God

Distribute the Soul Breakthrough workbooks.

Open with worship

Open with worship for half an hour and then share this scripture in the large group.

> **Therefore, if anyone is in Christ, he is a new creation. The old has passed away; behold, the new has come. (2 Corinthians 5:17)**

Pray over your time together that God the Father will do far more than you ask or think.

Watch Video 1

Small Group Discussion

Now gather in your small groups and go over the homework below and make sure everyone in the group understands the importance of doing the homework each day.

1. Invite Father God into your day and give the Holy Spirit permission to make you aware when you begin to move into old ways of thinking and feeling in response to familiar triggers. Then breathe deeply and lift your hands and invite Father God to fill you with His presence. Now journal what the Holy Spirit is saying to you.

2. Read several scriptures (feel free to read the scriptures below listed at the end of day seven).

3. Pray in your spiritual language for fifteen minutes or listen to worship music and sing to the Lord for fifteen minutes.

Below is a more complete explanation of the homework:

This week, **each morning**, invite the Holy Spirit to show you during the day when you are thinking and feeling the old broken ways. Give the Holy Spirit permission, during your day, to make you **aware** of what is controlling you.

When you are in a situation where you feel controlled by fear, anger, stress, depression, or insecurity, then lift your hands to Father God and say, "Father God, fill me with your Holy Spirit now. **I choose** to turn from anger, fear, stress, depression, _____to focusing on you." Take a deep breath and count to four. Now look at the situation filled with His Spirit and from the new creation that you are, and you will see things differently.

You have every resource in heaven and are a friend of God. Combine the physical act of lifting your hands while you invite the Spirit into your thoughts and emotions. This will break the old ways of thinking so you can focus on God. You can choose any physical act to combine with your words: clapping, smiling, looking up to heaven, or closing your eyes.

Remind them to do the homework.

Soul Breakthrough
Class Two
Hearing God's Voice

Open with Worship

Open with worship for half an hour and then share this scripture in the large group.

> **Therefore, if anyone is in Christ, he is a new creation. The old has passed away; behold, the new has come. (2 Corinthians 5:17)**

Pray over your time together that God the Father will do far more than you ask or think.

Watch Video 2

Small Group Discussion

Put a CD on with peaceful worship music or have the worship leader play for **ten minutes**. Each small group leader invites his or her group to rest in the Lord during this time.

Small group leader: Tell the people in your group to enjoy being with the Lord and receive His peace and love during this time. To help them with thoughts rushing in about errands or activities, tell them to picture pushing these thoughts away gently with their hand and focus on the Lord again.

Tell the people in your group, if they have difficulty with their minds wandering, to think of this scripture, **"The Kingdom of God is within you" (Luke 17:21).** Or picture the scene described in John 4:4-6: **"He came to a town in Samaria called Sychar... Jacob's well was there, and Jesus, tired as he was from the journey, sat down by the well. It was about noon. When a Samaritan woman came to draw water, Jesus said to her, "Will you give me a drink?"** Have them picture themselves in the Samaritan woman's place. Sit with Jesus and see what happens.

The group members can journal in the area provided in the work book if they receive something from the Lord. This might include a scripture, a picture, and thoughts from Him in their minds. Because the Lord is creative, He might choose to communicate in almost any manner.

After the ten minutes of resting with the Lord, ask each person to share about his or her week and how doing the homework has impacted them.

Go over the homework below again and make sure everyone in the group understands it.

Homework

1. Invite Father God into your day and give the Holy Spirit permission to make you aware when you begin to move into old ways of thinking and feeling in response to familiar triggers. Then breathe deeply and lift your hands and invite Father God to fill you with His presence. Now journal what the Holy Spirit is saying to you.

2. Read several scriptures (feel free to read the scriptures below listed at the end of day seven).

3. Pray in your spiritual language for fifteen minutes or listen to worship music and sing to the Lord for fifteen minutes.

Soul Breakthrough
Class Three
The Refining Process

Open with Worship

Open with worship for half an hour and then share this scripture in the large group.

> Therefore, if anyone is in Christ, he is a new creation. The old has passed away; behold, the new has come. (2 Corinthians 5:17)

Pray over your time together that God the Father will do far more than you ask or think.

Watch Video 3

Small Group Discussion

Have your small group sit quietly with the Lord for several minutes and ask Him to show them a painful situations in their past. Have them ask the Lord to show His purposes in this experience and how He has used, is using and will use that trauma or circumstance for good in their lives.

They can share this in the small group if they want. For those who choose to share, pray over them by inviting the Holy Spirit to show them that situation through His eyes.

> **And we know that in all things God works for the good of those who love Him, who have been called according to His purpose. (Romans 8:28)**

They can write down what He reveals to them in the workbook where space is provided.

Go over the homework below again, making sure everyone understands.

Homework

1. Invite Father God into your day and give the Holy Spirit permission to make you aware when you begin to move into old ways of thinking and feeling in response to familiar triggers. Then breathe deeply and lift your hands and invite Father God to fill you with His presence. Now journal what the Holy Spirit is saying to you.

2. Read several scriptures (feel free to read the scriptures below listed at the end of day seven).

3. Pray in your spiritual language for fifteen minutes or listen to worship music and sing to the Lord for fifteen minutes.

Soul Breakthrough
Class Four
Moving into Your Promised Land

Open with worship for half an hour

Watch Video 4

The format for the final class is different from all the other classes. After the short video, have the group leaders gather in the front facing each other to create a tunnel. As the team leaders are coming up to form the tunnel, explain that each person will be walking, by faith, through the Jordan into their Promised Land. Each person will go through the tunnel and receive prayer and impartation. Play the music or have the worship leader play while everyone is symbolically walking out of the wilderness, through the Jordon River, and into their Promised Land.

Remind the group before they go through the tunnel:

When God spoke to Joshua, He pointed out that the biggest enemies Israel would face when moving into the Promised Land were discouragement and fear, not armies or giants in the land. Faith in what God had promised was what was most needed, not fear.

> **Have I not commanded you? Be strong and courageous. Do not be afraid; do not be discouraged, for the LORD your God will be with you wherever you go. (Joshua 1:9)**

God's words to Joshua are the same words He gives to us. The only way to fight fear and discouragement is to be strong and courageous, to take hold of His Word, believe, and obey it.

Remind them to walk out of fear and discouragement and choose to be strong and courageous in the Lord as they walk out of their wilderness, through the tunnel (Jordan River) and into their Promised Land.

Meditate on these Scriptures

Below are a few more scriptures that you might memorize and study for they are saying something profound. The first scripture has been shared several times in this workbook, because when we really understand what is being said, we will be set free.

> **Therefore if anyone is in Christ, he is a new creation. The old has passed away; behold all things are new. (2 Corinthians 5:17)**

Do you want peace in your heart and mind, then throughout the day place it back on the Lord. Lift your hands to Him and say, "Father God, fill me with your Spirit."

> **You keep him in perfect peace whose mind is stayed on You. (Isaiah 26:3)**

Do you need strength throughout your day? Invite Jesus to strengthen you.

> **I can do all things through Christ who strengthens me. (Philippians 4:13)**

Would you like the God of peace to be with you, then read the scripture below? It tells you how.

> **Finally, brothers, whatever is true, whatever is honorable, whatever is just, whatever is pure, whatever is lovely, whatever is commendable, if there is any excellence, if there is anything worthy**

of praise, think about these things. What you have learned and received and heard and seen in me — practice these things, and the God of peace will be with you. (Philippians 4:8-9)

And finally the Apostle Peter explains how precious our faith is to our Lord.

An inheritance that is imperishable, undefiled, and unfading, kept in heaven for you, who by God's power are being guarded through faith for a salvation ready to be revealed in the last time. In this you rejoice, though now for a little while, if necessary, you have been grieved by various trials, so that the tested genuineness of your faith — more precious than gold that perishes though it is tested by fire — may be found to result in praise and glory and honor at the revelation of Jesus Christ. (1 Peter 1:4-7)

Jeremiah 29:11: For I know the plans I have for you, declares the Lord, plans to prosper you and not to harm you, plans to give you a future and hope.

John 10:10: I have come that they may have life and have it to the full.

Exodus 33:14: My Presence will go with you and I will give you rest.

Phil 4:13: I can do all things through Christ who strengthens me.

Isaiah 41:10: Do not fear, for I Am with you. Do not be dismayed for I am your GOD. I will strengthen you and help you. I will uphold you with My righteous right arm.

Proverbs 3:3-6: Trust in the Lord with all your heart and lean not on your own understanding. In all your ways acknowledge Him and He will make your paths straight.

Romans 8:28: And we know that in all things God works for the good of those who love Him, who have been called according to His purpose.

Matthew 11:29: Come to Me all you who are weary and burdened and I will give you rest. Take My yoke on you and learn from Me. For I am gentle and humble in heart and you will find rest for your souls. For My yoke is easy and My burden is light.

Isaiah 44:3-5: I will pour water on the thirsty land, and streams on the dry ground; I will pour My Spirit on your offspring, and My blessing on your descendants. They will spring up among the grass like willows by flowing streams. This one will say, 'I am the LORD's...and another will write on his hand, the LORDS's.

Philippians 3:12-14: Not that I have already obtained this or am already perfect, but I press on to make it my own, because Christ Jesus has made me His own. Brothers, I do not consider that I have made it my own. But one thing I do: forgetting what lies behind and straining forward to what lies ahead. I press on toward the goal for the prize of the upward call of God in Christ Jesus.

Philippians 4:8-9: Finally, brothers, whatever is true, whatever is honorable, whatever is just, whatever is pure, whatever is lovely, whatever is commendable, if there is any excellence, if there is anything worthy of praise, think about these things. What you have learned and received and heard and seen in me—practice these things, and the God of peace will be with you.

1 Corinthians 9:24-27: Therefore, since we are surrounded by so great a cloud of witnesses, let us also lay aside every weight and the sin which clings so closely, and let us run with endurance the race that is set before us.

Luke 17:21: The Kingdom of Heaven is within us.

Matthew 7:7: Ask and it will be given.

Matthew 10:27: My sheep hear My voice.

Hebrews 11:6: Without faith it is impossible to please God, because anyone who comes to Him must believe that He exists and that He rewards those who earnestly seek him.

Psalm 37:7: Be still before the LORD and wait patiently for Him.

Isaiah 30:15: In returning and rest is your salvation. In quietness and trust is your strength.

Job 23:10: But He knows the way that I take; when he has tried me, I shall come out as gold.

Zechariah 13:9: I will put this third into the fire, and refine them as one refines silver, and test them as gold is tested. They will call upon My name, and I will answer them. I will say, 'They are My people'; they will say, 'The LORD is my God.

Psalm 19:9-10: The judgments of the Lord are true and righteous altogether. More to be desired are they then gold, than much fine gold.

Job 23:10: But He knows the way that I take; when He has tried me, I shall come out as gold.

Psalm 66:10: For you God, tested us, You refined us as silver.

Proverbs 25:4: Remove the dross from the silver, and a silversmith can produce a vessel.

Malachi 3:3: He will sit as a refiner and purifier of silver; He will purify . . . and refine them like gold and silver.

2 Corinthians 10:4: For the weapons of our warfare are not of the flesh but have divine power to destroy strongholds. We destroy arguments and every lofty opinion raised against the knowledge of God, and take every thought captive to obey Christ.

Galatians 5:16-18: So I say, walk by the Spirit, and you will not gratify the desires of the flesh. For the flesh desires what is contrary to the Spirit, and the Spirit what is contrary to the flesh. They are in conflict with each other.

Ephesians 4:22: Put off your old self, which belongs to your former manner of life and is corrupt thru deceitful desires, and be renewed in the spirit of your minds, and put on the new self, created after the likeness of God in true righteousness and holiness.

Joshua 1:9: Have I not commanded you? Be strong and courageous. Do not be afraid; do not be discouraged, for the LORD your God will be with you wherever you go.

Please visit our website at
soulbreakthru.com

Now available in paperback and e-book

The first book in

The Old Tree Series

The Old Tree

Tricia Martin

THE ADVENTURE BEGINS

The Old Tree…a doorway to other lands and
extraordinary kingdoms…a new powerful friend…a
great battle rages.

Mike is bored with his summer vacation and meets a new neighbor, Mari.
Together, with a loving and powerful friend, Joshua, they crawl into an
extraordinary tree and are surprised when they find the Old Tree is a
doorway into a wonderful kingdom. When Mike and Mari return home,
they discover a terrible battle raging. They must join their friend Joshua in
saving their world from their enemy, Sitnaw.

Now available in paperback and e-book

The second book in
The Old Tree Series

The Land of Bizia

Tricia Martin

A VERY BUSY LAND

The Old Tree…a doorway to a busy land, an evil lord,
beautiful, underground caverns, and a sinister plan
waiting to be discovered.

Mike and Mari find themselves in a world that's on the verge of
destroying itself through busyness. With the help of their loving and
powerful friend, Joshua, can they rescue the people of Bizia and
bring them back to the values, peace, and fun they once knew?

Now available in paperback and e-book

The third book in
The Old Tree Series

The Kingdom of Knon

Tricia Martin

AN UNDERWATER KINGDOM IN CHAOS

The Old Tree…a doorway to an underwater kingdom
in chaos, a beautiful princess needing to be rescued…a
book that holds the key.

The Book has been stolen! That rare gift from the Creator to the people of
the Kingdom of Knon when first their kingdom had been made. Now
everything has changed in Princess Aria's beautiful kingdom, and
confusion, chaos, and fear rule her land.

Joshua brings Mike and Mari to the underwater kingdom to join with
Princess Aria. Together, they must travel into space to defeat evil Sitnaw's
plan to rule the Kingdom of Knon.

Now available in paperback and e-book

The fourth book in
The Old Tree Series

The Mild, Mild West

Tricia Martin

A GHOST TOWN AWAITS

The Old Tree…a doorway to a ghost town, talking
quail, and evil Sitnaw prowling around a town of
innocent families.

Mike and Mari arrive in the middle of the night in front of the Old Tree
where Joshua is waiting. They join Mie, a member of a race of warrior
beings from Joshua's realm, and journey into an Old West town to help
in an important rescue. Young people have been suddenly
disappearing from their families. Mike, Mari, Mie and Joshua join a
group of quail who are eager to defeat the sinister plans of Sitnaw.

Now available in paperback and e-book

The fifth book in
The Old Tree Series

Into the Night Sky

Tricia Martin

A FLIGHT INTO SPACE

The Old Tree…a voyage into space in a horse-drawn
carriage…a search for a special hat…a temptation.

Mike and Mari befriend a British boy, and all three find themselves in
the middle of the night on Philip's street. On Philip's front lawn is a
carriage attached to two fiery horses waiting to fly them into space to
search for an extraordinary hat that has been stolen from the land of
Bizia.

Now available in paperback and e-book

The sixth book in
The Old Tree Series

Arabian Lights

Tricia Martin

JOURNEY TO A BARREN DESERT LAND

The Old Tree…a doorway to a barren desert…a band of
thieves…an oasis…a lost baby.

Mari's father and his sister, as children, discovered the old tree for the
first time. When they walk through the other side, they find themselves
in a barren desert. An important child needs their help to restore his
purpose.

Now available in paperback and e-book

The seventh book in
The Old Tree Series

One For All and All for One

Tricia Martin

LANDS AND KINGDOMS IN PERIL

The Old Tree…where they travel through
time…Abe Lincoln shows up as a child…hope is
lost, and they must restore it.

All the worlds, lands, and kingdoms are on the verge of being
destroyed by evil Sitnaw. Joshua asks Mike and Mari to travel
back in time to solve this problem. They must find Abe Lincoln
when he was a child and convince him to join with them to
prevent the destruction of all they value.

The Intimate GOD

Tricia Martin

Come on an adventure with the Creator and discover His desire to have an intimate and personal relationship with you, His child and friend. Our heart attitudes can create static between us and our Beloved. As we learn to quiet our hearts and minds, we are able to rest in the arms of God.

ABOUT THE AUTHOR

Tricia Martin is the author of nine books including *The Intimate GOD*, and a seven book children's series entitled *The Old Tree Series*. She holds a Master of Arts degree in counseling and belongs to the Society of Children's Book Writers and Illustrators. A frequent exhibitor at the Christian Home Educators Association of California (CHEA) and Great Homeschool conventions, Tricia continues to be passionate about helping children fall in love with Jesus through reading.

Tricia's latest teaching, **Soul Breakthrough,** was developed to enable God's children to step into their Promised Land and walk as **new creations in Christ**. Because of the significant impact this class has had on people's lives, she created the **Soul Breakthrough** workbook.

She also oversees the prophetic ministry at Vineyard Community Church in California, and teaches a number of classes including: Intimacy with God and hearing His Voice, and Biblical Dream Interpretation.

She has been married to her best friend, Steve, for over forty years, and their favorite child is their only son, Mike.

Made in the USA
Monee, IL
27 May 2021